G000141521

Swan fc
Seasons

Poems by Richard Bonfield

To Katie

wishing you a lovely XMAS
e a very happy millenium

All bright blessings!

Richard
x
Dec 1999.

COYPU PUBLICATIONS

COPYRIGHT

First published in 1997 by
COYPU PUBLICATIONS,
26 Portway Square,
Norwich A Fine City
NR2 4QQ
with the help of The Incubators.

A CIP record for this publication is available from
The British Library.
ISBN   0 9521016 1 0

Printed in East Anglia by
The Modern Press on Reprise
acid free re-cycled paper.

Typeset in Berkeley
(Medium Italic, Bold and
Extra Bold).
Formatted in Quark
Xpress, using Mac
hardware. Illustrations
digitised and retouched
using an Agfa Scanner
and Adobe Photoshop.

FOREWORD

This, my second collection, was first seeded, sometime before I started **A Bestiary** in the poem **First Fire** which was the only worthwhile poem I wrote whilst on The Enterprise Scheme as a writer and poet back in 1987. I was sitting in the back room of my flat at the fag-end of Autumn with my small wood fire blazing when I disappeared into the timeless zone and returned with something that ultimately made the whole year worth while. Other seasonal poems had been planted at intervals whilst working on my first collection, and I realized when the fog had cleared a few months after **A Bestiary** came out that I had the makings of a small copse, if not a forest. The resulting collection has grown in the ensuing years, and this is my signposted path through **The Wood of Wyrd.**

For a year or two I worked on the idea of a collection to be entitled **Lower Light** as I had produced several poems about Autumn; but, as poems took root in other seasons, I began to think that I was probably on board for the whole journey; a probability that hardened to a certainty when I realised that the poem **Swan for all Seasons** also afforded me a title to encompass the whole.

The Seasons are one of our most powerful metaphors for life which is why, although they are an old chestnut, the theme is returned to again and again. This is my take on the old saw and, whilst some might accuse me of 'doing a Nigel Kennedy', it is my own response. This is how, in varying degrees, the seasons have affected me and, hopefully my response will find echoes in the reader's experience.

The collection takes you on a journey through the seasons, but also takes you on a journey through my life and the life of everyman/woman. I do hope that you will enjoy the trip. Ultimately we all travel the same path from forceps to stone. This is simply the view of one pilgrim from the long and winding road.

Richard Bonfield: Oak Villas, Norwich A Fine City June 1997.

P.S. I have included a few animal poems from **A Bestiary** as I felt that they would benefit from being seen again in a different setting.

ACKNOWLEDGEMENTS

My thanks go to the respective editors of the following magazines in which many of these poems first appeared (or are soon to appear):

Cadmium Blue, Candelabrum, The Country Standard, Envoi, Exile, First Time, Foolscap, The Frogmore Papers, The Haiku Quarterly, Helicon, Iota, Outposts, Peer Poetry, Pennine Platform, Poetry Nottingham, Poetry Monthly, Still and Weyfarers.

The poem **Haiku for a Robin** was first broadcast on Radio 4's Natural History Programme in 1993; **Hiroshima Memory** was an Editor's choice in **Still** Issue 3 and **Beachcombers** is to appear in an anthology of 20th century poetry to be published by **The Red Candle Press** in Autumn 1998.

Many of the editors have been very supportive of the present collection and several waived subscriptions in order to contribute, so thanks once again for your faith and encouragement. Their names, together with all those who offered money, time, encouragement and/or skills are listed on the next page.

The illustrations throughout this collection are taken in the main from:

Knight's Pictorial Museum of Animated Nature, Knight's Pictorial History of England, Flowers of the Field and *The Woodland Trees of Britain* by The Rev W.C. Johns, **Outdoor Life** by P.N. Furnbank and last but by no means least Bewick's *justifiably famous* **British Birds.**

Other illustrations have been gleaned from a wide range of original sources and from modern anthologies of Victorian etchings. Posthumous thanks are due to the multitude of illustrators who have helped to breathe life into the present work. We will always owe these often unsung artists a great debt of gratitude, although great wood engravers such as **Tunnicliffe and Gibbins** have also emerged in this century to carry on the tradition. Unfortunately copyright precludes their use in the present volume, but I'm sure that their work will also become part of the culture. Photography can be a great art form; however, when capturing the essence of plants and animals something always seems to be lost in translation. The camera may never lie but I find that it is often economical with the truth when confronting nature; whereas the Victorian illustrators, their precursors and their 20th century counterparts manage to convey, at their best, the essence of the thing represented. It is almost more real in some cases than the creature or plant itself, which is why Bewick is often described as 'the poet of engravers'. He saw the natural world with a poet's eye, that is he saw through to the essence of things: the truth behind the veil. I hope that some of the images represented here will have a similar effect on the reader. "The truth...", to purloin a phrase from the present culture, "...is out there"!

Although I wasn't able to find original Victorian engravings for every single poem I did discover that my friend **David Atkinson** was, amongst other things (cricketer, thespian, small cigar smoker) a re-incarnated Victorian illustrator. This obviated the need for any seances and means that some of the illustrations are the work of a modern hand operating in the spirit of those evolving times. So the art of Victorian engraving (or, in his case drawings in an engraved style) is not dead; unless that is David is one of the living dead...?

Special thanks are also due to my girlfriend **Carol Turner** who provided me with the beautiful tree borders which decorate each page along with further illustrations in a Victorian style and to **Martin Cook**, the graphic designer who has helped me keep the egg warm through many nights slaving over a recalcitrant Apple. As usual I couldn't have done it without him. Thanks are also due to **The Blue Nile, Tim Buckley, Phillip Glass, John Tavener** and many others for providing backing vocals. The kettle was always on, **Swan papers** played their part and the pub was always just 10 scans over the horizon.

ACKNOWLEDGEMENTS

Finally *The Green House* in Norwich kept the faith *Peter Crowe* helped again in the antiquarian book department as did *The Tombland Bookshop* and *Besley's of Beccles*. And last, but by no means least I would like to thank *Claire Piggott* for her letters of encouragement, *Judith Pearson* and *Christine Hewson* for organising the reading at *The Little Theatre* in Leicester on September 12th, *Ted Hughes* for encouragement on The Haiku front and my mother and the rest of my family for once again providing the wherewithal to ensure that the ugly duckling of 4 years ago eventually hatched into the swan you see before you.

As I had supported a charity (*The Save The Indian Elephant Campaign*) when I published my first collection *A Bestiary – An Animal Alphabet* I felt that I would like to support another charity this time round. So, acting on the principle "Think Global Act Local" I decided that I would like to highlight an environmental body in The Anglian Region. And, as many people had mentioned the bird reserve at Welney near Wisbech I decided to contact the centre to see if I could be of some help: *Linda Butler,* the publicity Officer was good enough to send me a brochure documenting their activities. And, when I saw that they described themselves as being *A Place for all Seasons* I knew that I had discovered the charity I wished to take under my wing.

Bewick's mute swan which illustrates the poem Swan for all Seasons on page 1 is my *Swan for all Seasons* as it is the only swan which resides here all year (and many can be seen at Welney). But it is also home to a wide variety of other birdlife including The Russian Swans which visit every Autumn and can be viewed from the spectacular floodlit observatory.

I am very pleased to be able to support this charity and hope that interested readers will peruse the information included at the back of the collection and support the charity in their own way, either by visiting the reserve (or any of the others around the country) adopting a bird, becoming a Wetland Trust member or, hopefully all three!

Together we can make a difference, both now and in the future.

Incubators :
Listed below are all those who, by donating money, time, encouragement and/or skills have helped to hatch the ugly duckling and transform it into my *Swan for all Seasons.*

Paul Amphlett, Richard Austin, David and Rowena Atkinson, Kevin Bailey, Bernard O' Brian, The Bonfield Family, Margaret Buckel, Margaret Bultitude, Linda Butler, Sara Clark, Jan Collins, Martin Cook, Peter Crowe, Eric Duporge, Andrew Elsegood, Amanda Jayne Glenn, Helen Gordon, Maria Guerten, Cherri Harrison, Felicity Hartley, Judith Havens, Alan Helsdon, Christine Hewson, Eileen Hogg Annie Holgate, David Holliday, Martin Holroyd, Ted Hughes, Doreen Ives, Jayadeva, Ai li, Gerry Lucioli, Ann Elliott-Marr and John Marr, Len McCarthy, Mary and Roy Maclean, Wolf Malucha, Terry Marshall, Mary Micklewright, Roz Myhil, Minka Nicholson, Shelagh Nugent, James Pearson, Judith Pearson, Margery Peverley, Claire Piggott, Barbara Richards, Danene Rogers, Joan Rees, Heather Stallwood, Keith Smith, Tigger and all at the Green House, Peter Geoffrey Paul Thompson, Alison Towndrow, Alison Tremeer, Joan Tuckley, Carol Turner, Zoe Wanamaker, Catherine Williams, Ted Williams, Ian Wright, Jean Young and Tasmin Young

David Atkinson provided the Swan pagination and the illustrations on pages 4, 5, 6, 11, 14, 35, 36, 50, 61, 64, 83, 114 and 130 (snow background).

Carol Turner provided me with the tree borders and the illustrations on pages III, 17 and 131.

The actress *Judith Pearson* read with me at the fund-raising evening staged at The Little Theatre in Leicester on September 12th 1997 and my musical friend *Alan Helsdon* provided the "Swansongs"

Many thanks to *Judith Havens* for proofing an at times intractable manuscript.

I hatched it *"With a little warmth from my friends".*

CONTENTS

CONTENTS

87
AUTUMN

119
WINTER

WWT

Dramatis Personae

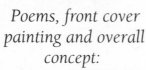

Poems, front cover
painting and overall
concept:
Richard Bonfield

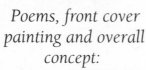

Graphic Design, text layout and
scanning:
Martin Cook

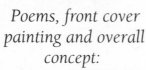

Photography, swan pagination and
various illustrations in a Victorian style:
David Atkinson

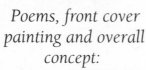

Tree borders and
various illustrations
in a Victorian style:
Carol Turner

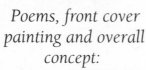

Best Cat:
Paddy

Swan for all Seasons

Poems by Richard Bonfield

For Carol, 'a woman for all seasons'

HAND MADE IN NORWICH
a fine city

Spring

Summer

Autumn

Winter

Swan for all Seasons

A primrose
Peering from a floating snowdrift;

A saxophone
Blowing in an autumn gale;

A cloud of incipient summer lightning;

An ivory bookmark
In a Winter's tale.

The Poet and the Blackbird

My gold-nibbed pen
And this famished Blackbird
Both scratching a living
On Winter's empty page.

Beachcombers

Walking in each other's minds
Along the beach,
We hope to find
Something that will tell us why
Love drifted off
And left us blind.

Walking in each other's minds
Across our lives,
We hope to find
A bottle with an ancient rhyme
That tells us why
We were unkind,

And walk along this shell-lined shore
In search of pearls we had before.

The tide drifts out
And leaves us dry,

We dream beneath a capsized sky

And walk inside each other's minds

Wishing we had been more kind.

Look...! at the Snow

Today I took time out
Just to unwind.

The snow came down
After bright sunlight,
Moving in strange combinations.

Apart from a few runners
I had the world to myself.

" Look,"...I tried to say to them —

"Look...!.at the snow."

But...of course...no one was listening.

They just stared at me
As they ran past,

Thinking

"Who is that mad bugger

Whispering?"

Sacred snow

Outside my window
Flakes of six-sided silence
Cover the earth with a tilth of stars.

Oberon's Dream

If I could
I would make hail
Into a diamond necklace

Then watch it melt
And splash your breasts.

Fir Cone

The fir cone
Opens its shutters
Like a breathing pagoda –
Snaps them shut in the crystal wind.

Snowdrop Triptych

Snowdrops arrive
Like a rumour of Spring
A paler precursor
Of "Wonderful things".

Great aunts with hankies
They whisper in white
That once they were bluebells
Who danced through the night.

Flowering snowdrifts
By yew-tended graves;
Reminders of chapels
Where love was displayed;
Snowdrops have sprung from the unyielding earth
Like manna dispensed from a crusader's purse.

Norfolk Snowdrops

Crystal flowers from crystal seeds,
Winter's wild epiphanies,

Rooted snow in woodland space
Carillons of perfumed grace,

Pearls from Winter's haûte-couture
That freckle Blakeney's storm-tossed shore,

Snow's pastiche of coming Spring:
The season borne on vernal wings.

Looking

Looking into every new woman's face
I build a fragile dossier of compatibility.
From every new woman's smile
I construct a photofit life
As if a face and a figure were all that I needed;
As if from one anonymous skull
A few strands of auburn hair
And the smell of roses
I could sculpture a perfect wife.

Girl with a Pearl Earring

The smile slips from her painted lips
As she watches you across the lounge;

A charming girl from a small Dutch town
Whose eyes still follow you around

As if to say, "When can we meet?
I shan't be long, I'll be discreet.

When Vermeer's gone
    we'll paint the town.
Just hand me down, just
    hand me down

Then walk with me
Through my charming
    town."

Not

I fancy her –
She fancies Not.

She fancies me –
I fancy Not.

And so the world keeps shuffling round
With no one finding common ground

Except for Not who, all agree,
Is everybody's cup of tea.

No Luck at M & S

I gave you love
You gave it back —
It hadn't even been unpacked.

I took it back, but can't exchange —
It's unrequited;

What a shame.

Perfunctory

If that was a kiss,
So is dew
Melting on a lonely man.

Early Flowers Chapelfield Gardens, Norwich

Overnight
The Puritan park
Is stippled
With Cavalier needlepoint,

As if a wife had woken
With a golden thread,
Whilst her roundheaded husband
Wintered in bed,

Then greeted him with doublet and hose,
A Valentine threading his homespun clothes.

Crocuses

With their strong golden fingers
The crocuses are pushing up the roof of Winter
As if a great reclining Buddha
Were waking under the thawing stars
And gripping the hem of the flowering Earth.

Bright Mid-Winter Day
Pull's Ferry Norwich

No swans on the river today,
Only my bird-shaped thoughts
Cruising sun-flecked water.

Emperors

Glimpsed through winter mists
A swathe of glass-blown orchids:
A field of starlit chessmen
Glazed by the midnight sun.

Mole

Deep beneath the furrowed land,
The blind skin-opener
With its wicket-keeping hands
Is scrabbling through Stygian gloom,
Like a venerable scholar
In a starless room
Wading through his Stilton
With a Port-stained spoon.

Chandler's Moon
February 22nd 1996

Tonight
The moon's blinds are drawn
And I can only see a nail-paring of light
From my flat across the street,
While Venus shines like a five-and-dime
And all the stars are over-easy.

Late Snow

Snow is laid down regally
Like Walter Raleigh's cape:
Ermine stippled with aconites,
Violets flashing through lace.

1531.—Raleigh.

Book of Nature

Coiling from snow,
Primroses illuminate
The first verse of March,
The last page of snowdrops.

Spring Swallows

Spring is returning
On the wings of swallows:
Sky dolphins and cobalt Spitfires
Somersaulting in the cloud-tipped ocean

And through this avian commotion
Sunlight pours
Like fresh emulsion.

Snowdrop Moon

A snowdrop floating in the winter sky,
The roots of the moon
Go drifting by.

Spring on the Line:
A Nursery Rhyme

Deep down
Under snoring oaks
The dormouse is coiled in its thistledown cloak,
With its tail at a quarter to Christmas,
Its ears at half-past Autumn
And its thoughts in the kingdom of disembowelled stoats;

Up above
In the kingdom of the polar bear
It's been an unrelenting Winter.

But listen now
And follow me down,
For deep inside a sundialled lair
There's an answerphone message from the Mad March Hare,

And underneath the waking oaks

A million flowers are clearing their throats.

Sycamore Seeds

Sycamore seeds are fallopian tubes –
Beautiful X-rays of trees in the nude;

Sycamore seeds are earrings of light –
Delicate wing-nuts that turn in the night;

Sycamore seeds are dragonfly husks –
Dryads of Summer that spin in the dusk;

And sycamore seeds are the keys on the ring
Of the door of the seasons

That opens on Spring.

Spring

Spring Docks

The other day
Spring drifted in
On a tide of flowers,

Unloaded her cargo
Of perfumed hours

And when the unloading was done
I watched the sailing of the Westward Sun.

Yorkshire Farmhouse Window

The only painting on the wall
Is a work by God
Entitled 'Spring'
Who also has three others
Under dust sheets in the wings.
They come out every year
And are hung successively,
But each time they are different
Though they frame the same blent tree,
And each time the light changes
It's God's Yorkshire that we see.

Yellow Laugh

The daffodils
Leap out from the brown palette of Autumn's remains —
Like a shout of joy in a Gentleman's club.

Lambs

A present posted in yesterday's Summer,
Autumn's gift to the year beyond,
A cumulus loaf from a snow-swept oven.
On the uplands of expectant Derbyshire
The Herdwick is licking a bleating rose
As Spring unwraps its gift to itself.

The Jackdaw

One of Fagin's spivvier boys
The jackdaw is a feathered kleptomaniac
From the roofscapes of the Gorbals;
Over-fond of other people's private joys
Sentimental baubles and Cartier toys.
But it has no sense of aesthetic taste
So that diamonds end up in the household waste.
It just enjoys collecting for collecting's sake
To feather its East End nest
In the very worst of eclectic haste;
So that Miros end up with Weeping Girls
And Woolworths rubs shoulders
With Fabergé pearls.

Wrens in Blossom,
Castle Acre Spring: 1996

In this Spring tree
A flowering of wrens:
A candelabra of tiny hearts.

Fishy Flowers

Bunched in their vibrant beds
Pansies and violets
Flicker like tropical fish
In a spring storm.

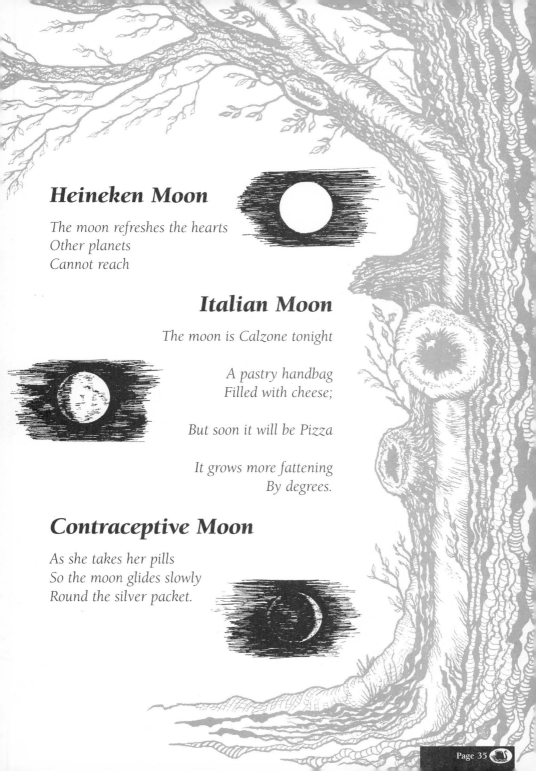

Heineken Moon

The moon refreshes the hearts
Other planets
Cannot reach

Italian Moon

The moon is Calzone tonight

A pastry handbag
Filled with cheese;

But soon it will be Pizza

It grows more fattening
By degrees.

Contraceptive Moon

As she takes her pills
So the moon glides slowly
Round the silver packet.

Bonsai Garden

In this morning dewdrop
Your whole garden
Shines.

The Globe
(For Sam Wanamaker)

The thatching glows like bearded gold;
The structure heaves and in its hold
The musings of a flickering man
Will burn across the watching land.
As Shakespeare rises from his sleep
The world contained inside his keep,
The characters inside his head
Are wakened from their vellum beds:
Bardolph, Pistol, Shallow all
 They flock towards the prompter's call.
  The ghost of Burbage bows his head
  And Will Kemp jigs on donkey's legs,
Leontes eyes his glass of wine
And Macbeth mouths the dagger's lines.
As players camp beside their fires
The playwright moves between the pyres
To test the waters of his thought,
Disguised as one his muse brought forth.
The cloak of tongues has spread the word
And leavened up the common herd;
The flag proclaims the play on view
And destiny awaits its cue.
The Folio is open now
And Ariel takes the nuptial bow:
A wind fills out the swelling scene;
The Globe returns from History's dream.

Secret Garden

My world's become a double-bed
With Spring erupting round the edge
And here my lover spreads her legs,
Her fingers flowering round my head.

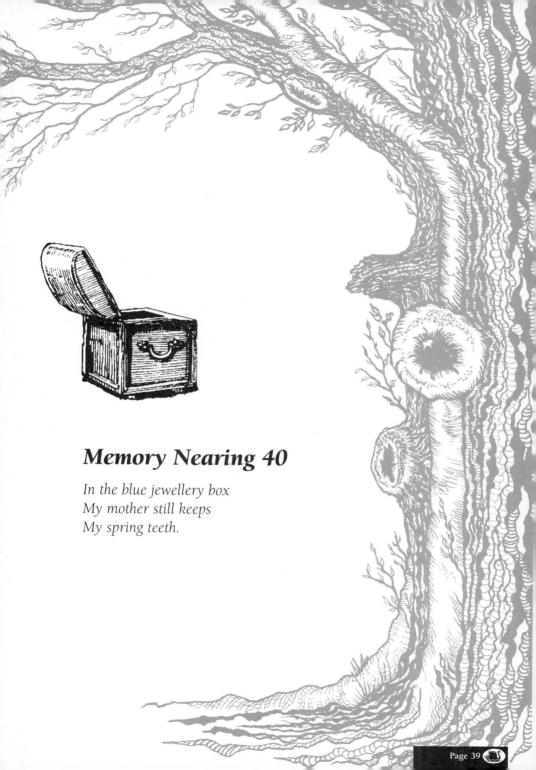

Memory Nearing 40

In the blue jewellery box
My mother still keeps
My spring teeth.

Blue Nile

A dream of Bluebells
Reminds me
Of Lapis-Lazuli;

The girl with the Nile in her palm-swept eyes.

Deer in Earlham Road Cemetery?

It was Bruce who told me there
   were deer in the cemetery

Hidden under small trees,
Blooming at dusk.

Somehow they had seeped through railings,
Painted themselves in with a velvety brush

To leave on the air
In the dew of the morning

A faint efflorescence,
Like Sweet Spirits laughing,

The scent of their passing,

The lawns tinged with Musk.

Cherry Blossom

The Cherry Blossom waits
For the Origami Master;
A day of perfect rain.

Spring Sunset

The eye of awareness
On a young girl's head,
Her Sari brushing over English fields.

If we could live and be as trees

If we could live and be as trees
We'd measure time in centuries

And have more time to feel the air,
The seasons passing through our hair.

If we could live and be as trees
We'd have more time to stop and stare.

If we could grow through light and air
We'd see the Green Man smiling there.

New Wine in Old Skins

Unfurling from the old stumps of many winters,
Fresh ivory blossom
Like milk-teeth gleaming in ancient gums.

Celtic Frost

That morning
After Irish rain,
A frosted shamrock
On my windowpane.

Spider

The spider is spinning a rose-window
In the morning wind;
An architect's blueprint
For a summer cathedral
Whose nave is lit by the warmth of the sun.

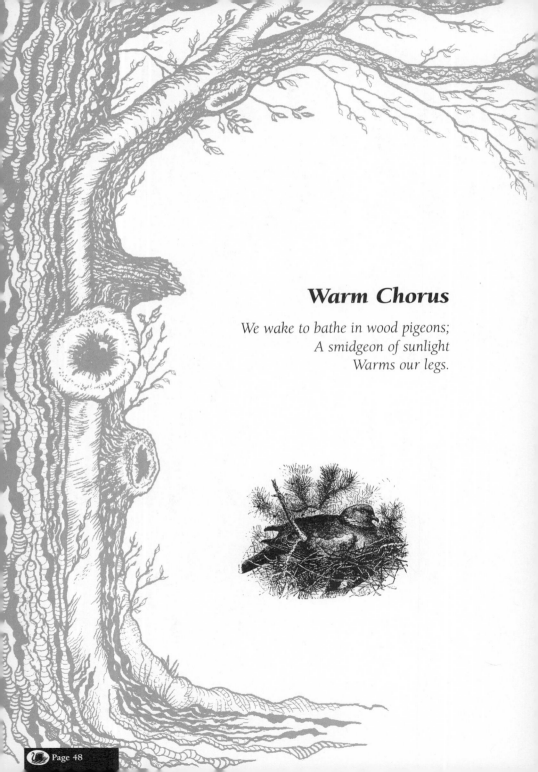

Warm Chorus

We wake to bathe in wood pigeons;
A smidgeon of sunlight
Warms our legs.

Summer

Solstice Sunday

Bat on willow
Village clock

Scent of tea
And key in lock

Sandwiches sliced nice and thin
Steeple's shadow
Lengthening

Peal of bells
And scent of hay

11 Played and won the day.

Then to the pub for ale and cheer
On this the turning of the year.

Wet Dream

All day
The man rests inside her
Like a rock pool
Left by passing waves.

Evening Carp

We sat at the head of the lake
And watched the great carp roll
In the lengthening evening,
Splashing in the sunset of our glasses.

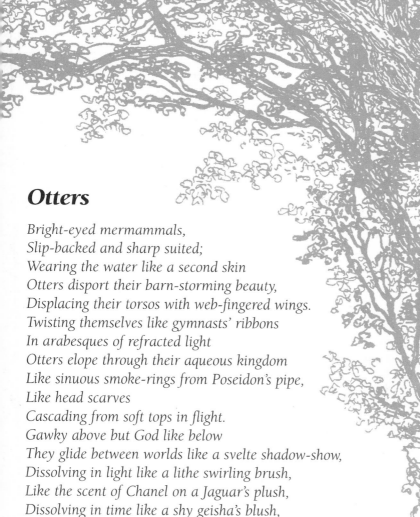

Otters

Bright-eyed mermammals,
Slip-backed and sharp suited;
Wearing the water like a second skin
Otters disport their barn-storming beauty,
Displacing their torsos with web-fingered wings.
Twisting themselves like gymnasts' ribbons
In arabesques of refracted light
Otters elope through their aqueous kingdom
Like sinuous smoke-rings from Poseidon's pipe,
Like head scarves
Cascading from soft tops in flight.
Gawky above but God like below
They glide between worlds like a svelte shadow-show,
Dissolving in light like a lithe swirling brush,
Like the scent of Chanel on a Jaguar's plush,
Dissolving in time like a shy geisha's blush,
Like a Cheshire Cat's grin
On a loch's midnight hush.

The Watchful Sandman

Love fades
Like forgotten telephone numbers:
The digits, once so meaningful
Are blurred within a week.

I put your photograph in the bin,
Sifted my soul from yours,
Took what could be recycled
To the memory-bank up the hill.

But even the cheerful dustman
Can't remove a dune of grief,

So I planted it with the marram grass of fortitude,
Erected the groynes of adversity,

Then I left it with the Watchful Sandman

By the ribs of a summer creek.

Foxgloves

Hatstands for gnomes
Gone to summer raves.

Dream of the
Cormorant Fisherman

In the night sky
My cormorant dives
Amongst shoals of stars.

Hiroshima memory

"The colours were so beautiful,"
Said the woman:
"Red, yellow, orange, green."

Poppies

On the fields of the Somme
Perennially bleeding
A red mist hovers.

Dragonfly

A flying boat
Of weightless glass
The stained-glass insect
Makes a pass
And tilts upon its fragile pins
To catch the Summer on its wings.

Phone Head

I picked up the telephone:
"No," she said, "I'm not dead,"
And all this time I thought
   that I'd been writing letters
To a stone head,
A basilisk of no emotions
Gazing out from hooded eyes
Across the shipwreck of our lives.

"Let's meet," she said,
"I know a place of greater safety,
It's a lovely island called friendship."

"Wonderful," I replied
"I'll be right over."

I put down the telephone,
Packed my griefs and my Raybans,
Climbed aboard the Ra of the future
And sailed to Easter Island instead.

Snails

Wandering homewards after summer rain,
I have often found snails
Fully-rigged on their silver seas
Leaving the ports of lamp-lit gardens
And I have stooped down
Like some fastidious Jain

Again
    and again
        and again
           and again

To plant them back in the comfort of gardens,
Safe from the anvils of moon-cracking thrushes
The churning wheels of brightly lit buses
And the crunching heels of unthinking lovers
Too busy fanning each other's ardour,
And too busy smoothing each other's pain
To notice the shipwreck of chestnut Armadas
Wandering homeless after summer rain.

Guide dog

A man's golden eyes
Doors of perception
On all fours;
Love in harness
The Labrador leads her master
Through invisible cities.

She waits
With the patience of Job
By rush-hour roads,
Leads her master
Through the red sea of impatient steel.

Curled at his heel
She is his Sign and Seal;

A symbiosis through patient osmosis;
The Ariadne who guides him through
The sound-filled tunnels of a sunless world.

Snail Memory

On this earthen bank
A sweetshop of dew-glossed snails
Takes you back to childhood days
When your world was a sylvan cornfield,
A feathered sea of golden waves.

On the contrary
we regretted everything

We had a café au lait
Spent a vile day near the Champs Elysées

You were angry,
I was sad,

The Eifell tower was raving mad.

We should have come for Le Weekend
Before we both went round the bend;

We should have come before as friends
— Paris is for starts not ends.

The Museum of Love

In The Museum of Love
There are many curiosities:
Terrible mistakes line the shelves
    in their cloudy jars.
They are all labelled,
All accounted for.
And in the Egyptian room lie the relationships
    he tried to save;
To embalm ardently beyond their rightful graves.
None of course are living in this catacomb of roses
Nobody ever comes –
Nobody ever visits –
The doors are sealed with lips of wax;
One cannot gain an audience by letter, phone or fax
For the Museum of Love is not open to the public.

Every so often a poem shines a torch,
The curator makes his rounds-
But the lips of wax are sealed,
Osiris has not risen
And the Museum of Love is silent
– There is nothing to report.

Summer Sunset

An egg
Veiled in evening's albumen,

Mae West's lips
Wreathed in smoke,

An apricot
Dropped in Hunza snow.

Shy Moon

*The moon is half hiding
Like a watchful geisha
By a temple pine.*

Ozymandias II

I felt you were my other half
The shadow on a summer lawn
Which, when I looked up
Showed me why
My present half was really born.

I felt that we were of a piece,
A sculpture joined by common clay
That, though it passed through many forms,
Had ruled a kingdom in its day.

I felt that time would find us out
Re-site us on a brilliant hill,
But though the forger plied his art
He did not have sufficient skill.

So now we lie in distant lands
Our pieces claimed by different hands,
And by the plinth where we once stood
The shards of love stretch far away.

Incontinentals

Rent-a-crowd –
Mad pigeons
Waddle and warble,
Zimmering inanely in the summer square
Posing before particularly imposing bins.

You can tell that their brains
Are tiny, – rare perhaps as a nubian pearl

They are so deliciously stupid
That you wonder if any of them know they are there.

Camera-hung you find them
From Basildon to Saint Mark's square
Incontinental tourists
Sans beaks, sans claws, sans brains, sans care.

Raspberry Recollection

Outside my grandmother's clock-shadowed lounge
The raspberries glowed in a Wimbledon sun;
And now, as I switch on my Magic-Lantern
A small boy flickers
Like a sepia phantom
Through a garden now grown faint with time —

Still brimming with raspberries in my mind.

Ignorance

A wasp
Banging on my bamboo blind –
Millimetres from an open window.

Butterfly Ball

Beside the old lock
This scented buddleia,
Bright with summer pilgrims.

Mementos

On the wall in her conservatory
Lie the bleached shells of yesterday's summers

Each shell drags up a different tide of memory,
Each wave drags up a different buoy –

And you can read the tides in her affairs with men
By the shells that remain when she's ended them.

Just pick them up and listen to the men:

Cockles and winkles
Stavros and Sven

Holiday Romances –
Remember them?

The Poet and the Bees

In the honeycomb of my head
Poems are distilled
From the wild flowers of adventure.

Swallows

Sycamore seeds
Dipped in lapis-lazuli;

Mackerel
Who've gained their wings;

Errant notes
From a summer chorus line;

Coathangers
For the autumn wind.

Sheepdog

A four-legged field radio,
A scampering chess-board
Alert to every whistling nuance,
The sheep-shadower
Slouches and sleuths
On invisible strings of obedience,
Dancing to the skylark of a man's fluted fingers;
And the sheep are nudged by waves of fear,
Bolstering together
In exact increments of terror
As the sheepdog quivers at the edge of instinct,
Balanced on the razor between hunt and herd,
Poised at the still point of the rustling heather.

Vaulting Ambition

A cloud caught on crags,
Delicate hooves supporting the swollen nimbus,
The sheep has ventured one meal too far
And cannot turn on the pencil-thin ledge.

Down below
An upturned hull of bones
Bears witness to the Grail of grass
Which lured this Herdwick up the path
And trapped it on the shelf of stone
Above the sheep-flecked fields of home.

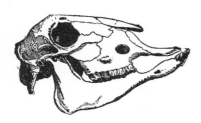

We Carved our Names

We carved our names into the tree
And hemmed them with a moated heart,
But as the tree grew rings of fate
The mildewed names were drawn apart;

And now a moat divides our lives,
Incised upon that summer pine
And nothing stops the widening sea,
The Continental Drift of Time.

Curlews

Above the sunrise
Curlews swirl;

Through thyme and space
Their cries unfurl —

And then they dip beneath the world
To nest on moons of speckled pearl.

Thunder Lion

The sky is out hunting:
Growling in the East
It rakes the damson evening
With golden zig-zag teeth.

Early Warning·

Slipped
Like a Tarot card
Into Summer's pack of days
Comes Autumn's early warning:

A crisper wind
A different light

And a sign-board man in a shroud of flowers
Crossing out the swallows in his Book of Hours.

Sex Tectonics

Saturday morning
And underneath the magma of the duvet
Islands are forming,
Collapsing,
Re-forming.

Tutankhamen's Lullaby

*(A verse inscribed on the sails
of a small golden ship plundered from the tomb
and never recovered until the poet discovered it
in his imagination.)*

*Now sleep – for Great Anubis
Who is Death's right hand,
Has steered your ship of heaven
Through our gates of sand.*

*Then wake – to find Osiris
Who is Dawn's best man,
Has moored your dhow of starlight
In his timeless land.*

Scarecrow

The scarecrow swings in the rain-drenched field;

A creature made of roots and wheels
Who cannot think, or hear, or feel;

And yet there's something in his stare
That makes me think there's someone there:

A sentinel at Summer's end
A Janus as two seasons blend.

Leveret

Summer has pulled up stumps
And a leveret sleeps
In the batsman's furrow.

Lower Light

As Summer opens the doors of Spain
I look to the leaves of Autumn,
Mottled and blotched as a fading hand.
Gently preferring the Lower Light
The dimmer-switch of the failing year.
For this is the season I harvest most

When the world is poised between Wine and Winter.

Autumn

September Haiku

Autumn declares itself
With a single leaf
Lost to the spin-bowling wind.

Autumn

The year's infirmity is now plain,
The bloom is burning,

Trees are burnished with weeping bronze;

And the elderly walk in their appointed season,
Viewing their lives through the guttering leaves
As they glimpse their extinctions
    in the brindled evenings.

Autumn Cactus Flower

*The cactus on my windowsill has just sent out this
Surprising emissary of*

Beauty.

*From deep in the heart of nowhere
The cactus has just exhaled this*

Delicate, purple-tinted

Sigh.

Bristol Docks

Down at the docks you can still smell the slaves

And the indigo

And sense that spirit of place

Umbered and silent

Ghosting down the riverway.

Wheel

We watch the generations pass –
All leaves are flesh
And then are grass.
The photos of the newly wed
Are lined up by the newly dead,
And outside leaves are falling fast;
The Summer of our years has past
And older now are you and I;
Within our hearts
The moon ticks by.

But soon dust will be flesh again,
The Bardo wheel has rings of grain;
Yes soon we will come forth again
To bloom afresh in snowdrop rain.

Benedictine Garden

In this autumn silence
The only sound
Is brush on leaves.

Autumn Light

Light streams like cider
From the quern of the turning sun,
Which crushes the crab-apple stars
One by sparkling one.

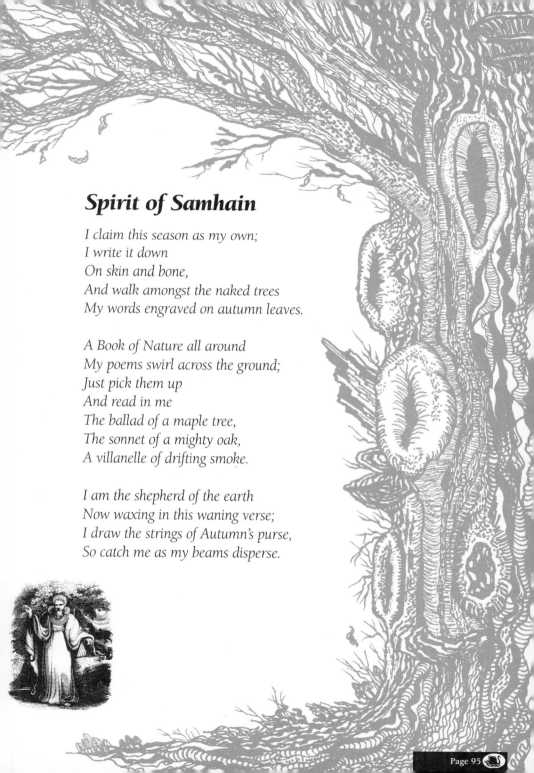

Spirit of Samhain

I claim this season as my own;
I write it down
On skin and bone,
And walk amongst the naked trees
My words engraved on autumn leaves.

A Book of Nature all around
My poems swirl across the ground;
Just pick them up
And read in me
The ballad of a maple tree,
The sonnet of a mighty oak,
A villanelle of drifting smoke.

I am the shepherd of the earth
Now waxing in this waning verse;
I draw the strings of Autumn's purse,
So catch me as my beams disperse.

Acorn

A ring around a severed finger –
Culloden's dreadful beauty
Lingers.

Acorns

U.F.O's in woodland glades
Land gently in an oak tree's shade.

The moon shines on their sylvan bed;
The Mother-Ship drifts overhead

Whilst up above the stars arc round
And glitter on her nut-swept downs.

Sweet Chestnuts

The sweet chestnuts have opened their castanet hearts
Revealing the souls of sea urchins;
Mahoghany earrings from Autumn's jewel box
Waiting to seed a grove of guitars,
A ruffled Armada of jostling lutes

Which the wind will pluck when they bow to the South.

Ninety-Niner

In his mother's oven
The ninety-niner bakes

Soaked in malted vinegar
Marbled through with hate;

For nothing's ever cracked
The old contender's skin

His hide is stegosaurian
Fiercely boiled in Vim

His atoms packed together
Like sardines in a tin;

And woe betide the oner
Who aims to chance his luck

In clashing with this conkeror
Whose hundredth scalp looms up.

October Massacre

Each October commences with this
rustling Passchendale:
The massacre of redoubtable leaf soldiers
By Autumn's implacable guns.

Karma

All the trees have surrendered;
They have given up their leaves
To the Season Inspector.
Only the Evergreens have escaped their tax on the sun,
But there's a file on them in a dusty boardroom
At least a cubit long,
And someone, somewhere
Wants an Evergreen table
To lay leaves on.

Fall

All along the road
The Summer's carapace
Glows.
The skin of breathing leaves
That cloaked the summer trees
Now gilds the autumn floor
With shrouds of wind-swept ore.
And Autumn's frosted breath
Enamelling the West
Has blown the swallows South
To swirl past Winter's jaws.

The Last Night of The Proms

In the great departure-lounge of Autumn
The evening chorus is disbanding.

Birds are seeking

Tangiers
            Malawi
Tahiti
            Maine

The compass is flowering in avian brains.

All species have their instinctual orders
That will carry them across autumnal borders;

Each take to their appointed sky-ways
And the rich fugue of Summer
Unravels,
Pavarottis and Te Kanawas
Drifting South
Leaving Robins to man the front of house
And Thrushes to busk in the bleak mid-Winter.

Transition

Wheeling like escaping leaves
The geese sweep over sleeping trees;

Their destination is the sun
That shines beyond the fowler's gun;

And as they flicker overhead
The Autumn turns its burning head

To watch the Summer passing by
As comets light the geese-filled sky.

Norfolk Fly-Past

Against the splendour of a Cotman sky
The brush-stroked geese go floating by,

And as their skeins bank overhead
The marsh below is flooded red;

And as they swing towards the sun
The fowler points his loaded gun

To scatter flocks like hand-tossed grain
Dissolving into autumn rain.

Red Squirrel Memory

I cup the leaf-flame in my head,

I hoard the haw-light,
Roaring red

And let it warm my autumn bed;

Through winter storms
I'm lantern-led.

Hedgehog

Autumn's pincushion,
The lovely moon-pig
Is teasingly, carelessly studded
With dead September leaves
As she shuffles down the catwalk
In an off-the-hedgerow number,
Her body liberally sequinned
With hundreds of glittering fleas.

Oak and Rowan (A Song)

Once
We bent together like a hedge
Woven by time and weather.
Once we were tenderly grafted,
An Oaken man and a Rowan wife
Married together by the hedge-maker's knife;
And though we are no longer spliced,
Although she leads a separate life,
Shadowy branches like severed limbs
Twine us across the tangled years;
And when she bends I feel her stir
For I felt complete inside of her,
And when I write I know she cares
For we're joined by ghosts, by rambling tares;
And though she's now a separate tree
She felt complete inside of me,
And though the hedge was torn apart
She left her roots inside my heart:
And when I see a Rowan tree
I feel her bend inside of me,
And when she sees an Oak in leaf
My roots entwine around her feet.

Autumn Sunset

A pumpkin
Blazing on a pagan fire;

A tangerine
Floating on an orthodox spire;

A golden apple
Called the sun

Sailing to Byzantium.

Badger

Painted with strokes of moonlight
The badger shuffles from the dark,

Like a part of the dark advancing,

The night-sky
Caught in ambling time-lapse.

Stars spark from its town-lit eyes
As this confederate of the constellations,
This charcoal woodsman
Prowls its monochrome kingdom,

Drifting down the path between dusk and dawn,

Melting with the morning
Like night fog
Lifting.

Weasel

A living stole
With Rayban eyes,
This Al Capone of svelte surprise
Slips furtively beneath the skies.

His mind is full of thoughts of eggs
Of scrambled voles and otters' heads,
And few elude this sylvan pro
Who guns for chicks in embryo.

Pumpkins

Cinderella's coaches stacked
Goblin heads in ziggurats

Discarded ball gowns from Versailles
Meteors trawled from leafless skies

Rusted buoys in hibernation
Viziers hats in dense formation

Basketballs from other stars

Candled skulls

Warm samovars.

Penny for The Guy (A poem for Victor Meldrew and Randy Newman)

Towards the end of October
Children stand on street corners
Asking for money to burn their grandfathers.

This is a peculiarly British institution;
Nowhere else in the world is such a bizarre form of
Euthanasia practised

But grandfathers are a burden,
A species beyond 'Our Ken'
Who go on and on about the Second World War
And how the world was so much better then.

And this seems as good a method as any
Of ridding the world of such redundant men,

And a lot less protracted than the earlier method
Of hanging, drawing and quartering them.

Second Coming
(A Poem for Ian Dury)

Deep amongst the autumn beds
A cordite Spring is underway

As Traffic Lightus Flareicus
Gives green to amber flower displays;

And Roman Candleisticus
Is puffing out her powdered blooms

As Action Parachuticus
Descends amidst the sparking gloom;

And all around the buds in flame
Remind us of the year that's flown,

As Jumping Jackististicus
Explodes beneath Aunt Ida's throne.

Standard Romance

We split up on Bonfire Night
I lit the green touch-paper of jealousy
And she disappeared
Trailing her flaming pearls.

In the morning,
Raking over the ashes
I found the Black-Box of our life.

Then I tracked her for weeks in another's gravity,
Followed the flight path of my rocket girl

Until I glimpsed her in a crater with a rocket man
Caught her 'in flagrante' with a passing Martian

And monitored her landing on a distant World.

Pheasant

In the corner of a deer-coloured field
This gilded flourish
On a scrap of moonlit vellum.

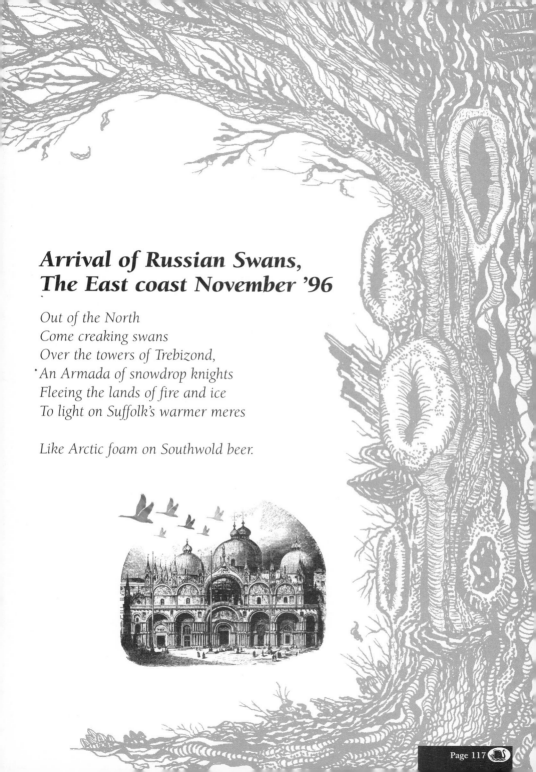

Arrival of Russian Swans, The East coast November '96

Out of the North
Come creaking swans
Over the towers of Trebizond,
An Armada of snowdrop knights
Fleeing the lands of fire and ice
To light on Suffolk's warmer meres

Like Arctic foam on Southwold beer.

First Fire

All of a sudden the wood catches hold
And the first fire of encroaching Winter
Leaps the long length of chimney
To breathe smoke at stars;
And warmth is born like a wave,
It flows into the bones as a vital wine.
Then, for the first time since March
The sun is on the hearth
And the moon is at the window.

Winter

December Bonfire

This bonfire
Unleashes Summer's diaspora
Into the swan-coloured wind.

Haiku for a Robin

In my emptied garden
This glass of autumn wine
Brims on Winter's table.

The Kingfisher

The Kingfisher
Erupts from charcoal
Like a Zen painting
Brushed to colourchrome life.
It has gathered the stray shades of Summer
Into a loom of Chinese lightning.

Caught in the rood of trees
Like stained-glass viewed from a spartan season
It roosts underneath the leaking chapel of Summer,

Flies

Like a water-colour fireball on a smoky autumn evening
Like a splinter of Nirvana in the gentle English snow.

Winter Sunset

Beached on the hill's horizon
The light leaks from the shipwrecked day

Until the silver moon of evening
Hauls the shipwrecked light away.

Priest in the Night

Unseen
The swan
Suddenly

Lifts

From the windblown page of Winter

To cup the moon with its white-gloved wings
And bless this world of sleeping things.

Winter Fox

The fox's brush paints its winter shadow
As it dips its tuft in aniseed moonlight
And leaves its scent for the trailing hounds
Who have stink-visions dreaming in their baying beds
Of steaming innards, dismembered heads,
Who can smell the prey in its reeking hose
As it leads them on by the frosted nose.
There's a smell consensus in their pell-mell pursuit
As they shadow the quarry with its aromatic loot
Until they lose it by a double-crossing coombe
As the fox swims over a howling moon.

Shape Shifter

(A dream of Avebury after
viewing a painting at
The Sainsbury Centre Norwich)

I walked beyond the painting's frame
To stand amongst the ancient stones
And felt the Iron Age stain my veins
Beside a tumulus of bones.

The painted wind beat on my head,
The air was filled with primal power,
And as the sun sank in the West
A figure climbed a painted tower.

It turned towards the setting sun
And then it raised a hawthorn wand,
And as I watched it changed its song

— The druid blurred — Became a Swan.

Comets

Night-flower
And burning swan,

Across the sky the comet
comes,

A migrant from the
depths of time,
Departing like a fading
rhyme.

Overhead a comet passes,
Interflora
Star to star.

A comet flaring
Soaring West
Everyman glimpsed
On an endless quest.

Winter Goldfish

Under the ice
The Goldfish glow
Like Christmas clementines
Wrapped in Snow.

hUnny I luv "U"

The eskimos hav 18 difrent names for snow
And todays snow waznt like any snow I now
But....in the absense of an eskimo
Piglet and I hav decided to call it
*   "snow"?*

I hav a similar problem with luv

The misstiks hav 18 difrent names for luv
And todays luv waznt like any luv I new
But... in the absense of a wizer pooh
Piglet and I hav decided to call it
"hUnny" with a capital "U"!

Ice House

In the Ice-House
A cargo of Winter

Sheared from the lake

A sleeping glass-harvest

Broken clouds for Summer drinks,

The shattered portrait of a Christmas sky.

Green Man

The Green Man grows so slowly
It takes a year to smile –

To it we're just bright shadows
Who are passing through the stile,

The stile that leads from birth to death
Before it's drawn an April breath,

The stile that leaps from birth to age
Before you've turned this frosted page.

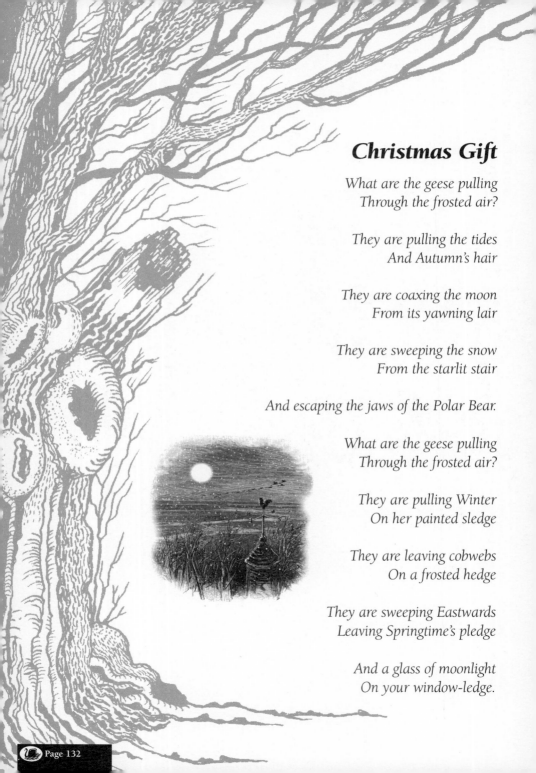

Christmas Gift

What are the geese pulling
Through the frosted air?

They are pulling the tides
And Autumn's hair

They are coaxing the moon
From its yawning lair

They are sweeping the snow
From the starlit stair

And escaping the jaws of the Polar Bear.

What are the geese pulling
Through the frosted air?

They are pulling Winter
On her painted sledge

They are leaving cobwebs
On a frosted hedge

They are sweeping Eastwards
Leaving Springtime's pledge

And a glass of moonlight
On your window-ledge.

I watched a single Snowflake fall

I watched a single snowflake fall
Against a frozen winter wall
And saw the beauty of it all,
The snow, the flake,
The oxen's stall.

A single snowflake in the sky,
The light that led the wise men by
And drew the shepherds from their sheep
To kneel at their Redeemer's feet.

I watched a single snowflake fall
Against a frozen winter wall
And saw the Saviour in His stall

The Flake that fell to save us all.

Message in a Bottle
(For Carol)

Walking in my new love's mind
I found a bottle with a rhyme.
I opened it
And mouthed the lines
"I'll walk with you
Because you're kind
And find in me a common shore
Where we can both discover more
Where we can comb beneath the sky
And know we know the reason why
Where pearls we find upon the sand
Are cupped between our loving hands
Like shells enclosing precious ore
The knowledge of an ancient law."
Walking in my new love's mind
I catch the scent of wind-blown thyme
And know that minds have matched a coast
From which to launch a spindrift boat
On which to sail far out to sea
Beachcombing for Eternity.

Box or Urn ?

Would I rather go in a Box or an Urn?
Would I rather be used for fertiliser
Or a breeding ground for worms?
A man I once knew
Finally found a use for his mother
As a doorstop.
It was, he said, the most useful thing she'd ever done
(Apart that is from producing a son).
Well I really don't know how I'd like to go
Though not bricked up à la Edgar Allen Poe.
I suppose it matters not
Buried or fried,
Exposed to Tibetan vultures under Himalayan skies
Drunk as Heinz ancestral soup by Amazonian tribes.
No I don't really mind how I'm married to Gaia;
It's my heart not my body that must play like a lyre.
I don't really mind if I'm rotting or singed

It's my soul not my corpse that must sing on the Wind.

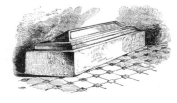

Ephemeral Juxtaposition

This blue door
Has been waiting all Winter
For the daffodils in the blue vase.

Swallows Know

Swallows know when it's time to go
But people seldom do.

(I thought there was going to be more to this poem
But swallows know when it's time to go
And poets seldom do).

WWT – AN INTRODUCTION

The Wildfowl & Wetlands Trust (WWT) was founded by the artist Sir Peter Scott, in 1946 on the banks of the River Severn in Gloucestershire. Sir Peter believed in bringing wildlife and people together for the benefit of both and the present staff of WWT are proud to carry on his work.

Today, WWT runs eight centres around the UK, including one each in Scotland, Wales and Northern Ireland. Each is different, but all are important for wetland wildlife. You can support the work of WWT by becoming a member or bird adopter (see following pages)

For the purposes of this collection, and as I live in the region I am going to concentrate on the work of The Wildfowl and Wetlands Trust at Welney near Wisbech in Cambridgeshire, but addresses and telephone numbers of the other centres are included at the end so that interested readers can contact the centre nearest to them. In any case visitors in the Anglian region will certainly be tempted to visit the other centres once they have sampled Welney's delights.

WWT Welney: A Place for all Seasons:
Hundred Foot Bank,
Welney, Wisbech, Cambs PE14 9TN UK
Telephone: Ely (01353) 860711

WWT Welney is a 1000 acre wetland reserve open to the public every day of the year except 25th December. The reserve boasts several modern birdwatching hides including the observatory which is heated and offers panoramic views over the main lagoon.

During the winter months the Welney Centre is famed for its breathtaking spectacle of thousands of wintering wildfowl which make for one of the greatest wildlife attractions in Europe: During these winter months approximately 5,000 wild swans from Iceland and Russia migrate to spend the winter on the reserve joining up to 20,000 wild duck from northern Europe.

The excellent hide system provides close-up views of many of these wild birds: From November to the end of

WWT – AN INTRODUCTION

February special Floodlit Swan evenings are held; visitors are taken to the heated observatory to view many of these birds and are given a live commentary about where the birds have come from, why many are "tagged" as part of research schemes and then watch as the swans are fed. These evenings can be booked by individuals or groups and it is quite an amazing and unique spectacle (many of the visitors coming long distances to view it).

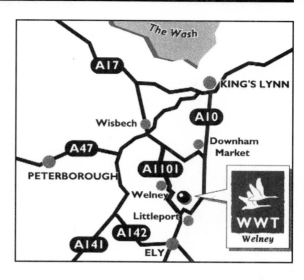

Spring and autumn is really change over-time with many birds arriving or departing for their summer breeding grounds or wintering sites. Throughout the summer waders, warblers and swallows live and breed on the reserve. Open from June to Sept is the summer walk a 2.5 mile route across the reserve which is lined with wildflowers and inhabited by butterflies and dragonflies.

Visitors to WWT Welney will be offered excellent reception facilities which include a gift shop offering binocular hire, The Wigeon Tea-Room (open from 10.30am-4.30pm offering hot and cold snacks) and a Display Hall with its exhibits and interactive computer. The education room is also available to school groups and offers a slide projector/overhead facilities and video (The room is also available for private hire and for children's parties). A Live video link brings close-up views of the nature reserve to the centre.

Toilets are situated within the visitor centre (please note there are no toilets on the reserve)

Picnic tables are located alongside the Visitor's Centre and by the Reedbed Boardwork. The trust regrets that no dogs are allowed on the reserve.

WELNEY – A HISTORY

If you look out over the Fen landscape today, dominated as it is by intensive farming, it is difficult to believe that 400 years ago this area was one of the largest wetlands in Europe.

Before drainage, the Fens were characterised by tracts of reedswamp with clumps of willow trees, large shallow lakes or meres and broad rivers meandering lazily through the countryside. The only settlements were on the few areas of land that rose out of the Fen - Ely, Chatteris and March were such places - actual islands within a sea of reeds. Life was hard within this area of constant dampness and fogs. Fear of disease and inundation from the sea contributed to making the Fen people a tough and hardy breed. Although the few areas of drier lands provided summer pasture, it was from the fen that a living was gained. There were plentiful supplies of fish and wildfowl, particularly in the winter time when their numbers were swelled by birds migrating from the north. Sedges and reeds were cut for bedding, peat dug in the spring was dried out for winter fuel and there were rushes and osiers for mat and basket making.

Although there were small scale attempts by the Romans and during the mediaeval period to tame the Fen, it was not until the 17th century that large - scale drainage of the Fens began. A key part of this drainage scheme was the Hundred Foot Washes, completed under the supervision of the Dutch engineer Vermuyden. Despite it being a massive undertaking, and the unsettled state of the country following the Civil War, the work was completed in 1651. Vermuyden created a flood alleviation scheme consisting of two parallel rivers, the Old Bedford River and New Bedford River, separated by a half - mile wide strip of flood meadow running for 22 miles.

When water levels rise in the River Ouse, threatening to overtop the banks, the sluice at Earith is opened and discharges water into the River Delph which in turn rises and floods the Washes. At times of heavy rainfall the Washes can be flooded from bank to bank. This water is then discharged back into the New Bedford at the Welmore sluice further downstream.

The regular winter flooding of the Washes resulted in the traditional Fen way of life - grazing cattle in the summer and wildfowling in the winter - being retained long after the surrounding Fenland was drained and put down to arable crops. The boom of the wildfowlers' punt-gun still resounded across the Washes long after the surrounding Fen became dry.

The retention of the wild nature of the washes resulted in them becoming one of the last remaining refuges for wetland wildlife after the Fens were drained. Sir Peter Scott, founder of The Wildfowl & Wetlands Trust, first came to the Hundred foot Washes in 1928 and was so taken with the winter flocks of wildfowl that he made many return visits. Links with the area were strengthened when Sir Peter came to live at Sutton Bridge lighthouse, near King's Lynn, in the late 1930s. With the anonymous donation of 100 acres of Washland in 1968, the Welney centre was opened in 1970 and Sir Peter Scott had realised another of his many dreams.

Since this time the Trust has continued to purchase further land and today the trust own almost 1,000 acres of the Washes, forming a complete, undivided block of land free from disturbance and traditionally managed. It was not only The Wildfowl & Wetlands Trust which recognised the conservation value of the Hundred Foot Washes; the Royal Society for the Protection of Birds and The Wildlife Trust of Bedfordshire & Cambridgeshire also own areas of land, such that today some 70% of the Washes are owned by conservation organisations.

THE SWANS

The Washes have always supported small numbers of swans during the winter months but it was not until the creation of refuge areas by conservation organisations, and greater amounts of agricultural waste left after harvest time out in the Fens, that numbers of wintering swans increased dramatically on the Washes. Between 1960 and 1965 the average number of Bewick's Swans wintering on the Washes was 171; during the same period Whooper Swans averaged five individuals. Over the past 30 years, number of swans wintering on the Washes have risen dramatically. In January 1990 there were 5,000 Bewick's Swans and 554 Whooper Swans using the secure night-time roosts on the Washes and feeding out on the Fen fields during the day.

Mute Swan
Large size
Orange bill with a black knob at the base
S shaped neck
Average weight 11.9kg

Although it is one of the heaviest flying birds in the world, the mute swan is a universal symbol of grace and beauty. With its pure white plumage and orange bill it is one of our most striking resident birds. Mute swans tend not to move far from their breeding areas - those that winter at Welney are mainly local Fen birds which come together to take advantage of the available food and security of the Reserve.

Although its name may suggest that the Mute Swan is silent, if you listen carefully you may be able to hear a low guttural grunt that is the Mute Swan's call.

Whooper Swan
Slightly smaller than Mute Swan
Angular head shape
Pointed wedge shaped area of yellow on the bill
Average weight 9.5kg

The Whooper Swan takes its name from its loud whooping call which along with the similar call of the Bewick's Swan will be heard throughout your visit to Welney. The Whooper Swan breeds across much of northern Europe and Asia, tending to nest not quite as far north as the Bewick's Swan. Their most westerly breeding area is Iceland and it is from here that the Whoopers that winter in Britain come. Although small numbers of Whooper Swans remain in Iceland throughout the winter, congregating around hot thermal springs, the bulk of the population winters in Ireland and Scotland, while smaller numbers winter in England. At Welney, numbers can reach 1000 individuals, the largest herd of Whooper Swans in England and Wales.

THE SWANS

Bewick's Swan
Smallest of the three species
Rounded head shape
Rounded area of yellow on the bill,
but less yellow than the whooper
Average weight 6.4 kg

The Bewick's swan was named after Thomas Bewick, the 18th century engraver and ornithologist. Although it is the smallest of the three swan species present at Welney during the Winter months, the Bewick's Swan makes the longest journey to reach us. They breed on the tundra of Arctic Russia and fly some 2,500 miles to reach their wintering areas in Britain. This migration takes about two months, with favoured stopping - off points along the Baltic coast, northern Germany and Holland. Some Bewick's Swans overwinter on the Elbe estuary on the German coast and many remain in Holland. However, should cold weather strike continental Europe these Bewick's will stream across the North Sea to join those which arrived earlier in the winter.

The Hundred Foot Washes have the largest concentration of wintering Bewick's Swans in Europe, while smaller numbers overwinter at The Wildfowl & Wetlands Trust Centres at Slimbridge and Martin Mere, with occasional parties also appearing at Arundel and Caerlaverock.

Each Bewick's Swan has an individual bill pattern, as individual as our own fingerprint. Whooper Swans also have individual bill patterns although it is less obvious in the Bewick's. If you look at the Bewick's and Whoopers in front of the main observatory you will easily be able to pick out the three main forms of bill pattern, known as **"Yellowneb", "Darky" and "Pennyface"**

Experienced swan - watchers can identify certain individuals just by looking at their bill patterns and will expectantly await the arrival of their favourite swans in the autumn.

Ringing

To further aid identification of individuals some Bewick's and Whooper Swans have been fitted with leg rings. These are made of a hard - wearing plastic and are inscribed with a sequence of two or three letters, with each swan having its own sequence. The ringing of swans is vital to enable identification of individual swans in the field and to build up a picture of their movements and life history.If you notice a ringed swan during your visit please let one of the wardens know and they should be able to give information on when and where a particular bird was ringed.

THE SWANS

Family Life

After hatching (the Bewick's on the Artic Tundra, the Whoopers just below the Artic Circle in Iceland) the cygnets have only a short period of time before the arrival of winter weather forces them to make their long journey south. Their first year of life will be spent in close proximity to their parents. Unlike some migratory birds which are born with their migration routes genetically instilled within them, swan cygnets learn their migration routes from their parents.

Cygnets are recognisable by their grey plumage and lack of yellow on the bill. Mute Swan cygnets have brown plumage. They will not stray too far from their parents, flying out together to feed in the Fen fields and roosting at night never further than a few metres from each other. Sometimes extended families occur and this has been confirmed by studying ringed families. The extended family usually consists of the previous year's young tagging along with the new family. Second-year Bewick's are identified by having a few grey feathers remaining on the head and neck of their otherwise white plumage. Whooper and Bewick's Swans on average have two young although in exceptional circumstances six young have been seen in a family group, although it is known that adoption does occur. Look out for family groups on the main lagoon at Welney either roosting or swimming together. The swans reach breeding maturity at the age of four years and they will then find a mate. They will stay as a pair for life, only finding a replacement if the original mate should die, although there is a record of a pair separating and the female finding a new mate. Pairs of swans can often be seen in courtship where they will come together, almost touching their heads and necks. Not all contact between swans is so passive and occasionally aggression breaks out amongst them. Usually this is just bluff with a lot of noisy calling and wing-flapping although it can result in blows being struck.

Of the three species of swan at Welney it is the Whooper Swan that is the most dominant, with the Bewick's being less so. The Mute Swan is totally passive toward the other two species and will back down in any dispute with the Whoopers or Bewick's.

Feeding of Swans at Welney

To provide a spectacle in the main lagoon and to draw the swans up close to the observatory to study bill patterns and read leg-rings, the swans are fed periodically through the day with grain and also potatoes are put out on the edge of the lagoon. This is only a token feed which does not sustain the swans; there is a wealth of food in the form of potatoes and sugar-beet left on the fields after the main crop has been harvested out in the Fens. The swans will also graze on the fields out in the Washes and feed on water weeds in the lagoons, ditches and ponds.

OTHER WILDLIFE

Other Wildfowl at Welney

The many pools and areas of shallow flooding at Welney provide just the right conditions for many species of wildfowl. Most of the hides at Welney should give good views but as a rough guide the Observatory will give good views of Pochard, Mallard, Pintail, and Tufted duck, while the Buxton and Allport Hides tend to play host to the shier species such as Teal, Gadwall, Shoveler and Wigeon.

Geese

The Hundred Foot Washes do not attract large numbers of geese, the reasons for which are not exactly clear. Through the winter months a flock of up to 400 Greylag Geese can be seen at Welney, intermingled with which can be small numbers of Pink-footed Geese (Greylags also have pink feet) and the occasional White-fronted and Bean Geese.

More Winter Wildlife

While looking at the massed flocks of duck out on the Washes you may see mass panic occurring with large numbers of birds flying up into the air or cascading into the nearest area of open water. This behaviour could be the result of a predator being in the area, possibly either a local Sparrowhawk or a visiting bird of prey. Hen Harrier, Merlin, Peregrine and Short-eared Owl can all be seen from time to time through the winter.

As you walk along the Screenbank Walk going from hide to hide, keep an eye out for many of the small birds that make their home at Welney. Reed Buntings can be seen, along with members of the tit family, and flocks of House Sparrows are worth a second glance as Tree Sparrows are regularly seen through the winter. Mixed flocks of finches feed on split corn and seeds, and in hard weather Bramblings join the Chaffinches, Goldfinches and Greenfinches

SEASONS AT WELNEY

Welney in Winter

The relatively mild winter conditions experienced in Britain, owing to its presence on the western edge of Europe, makes it a favoured destination for many species of birds escaping the cold of eastern Europe and northern Asia. Many thousands of wildfowl cross the North Sea to spend the winter on the Hundred Foot Washes. At Welney the presence of shallow - water areas for roosting, a secure reserve free from disturbance and a wealth of food in the form of potatoes and sugar - beet waste left on the fields after harvest provide perfect conditions for wintering wildfowl.

Spring and Autumn at Welney

The two parallel rivers of the Hundred Foot Washes are used as a flyway for many species of birds. The many pools and areas of shallow water and mud attract these birds to Welney to rest and feed before continuing their journeys north to breeding grounds in the spring and south to wintering areas in the autumn. If conditions for migration are favourable, the sheer variety of birds can be astounding, ranging from small warblers through to wading birds, terns and birds of prey.

One of the most varied groups of migrants at Welney are the waders which find the wetland conditions much to their liking.

Wading birds at Welney

The Observatory, Buxton and Allport Hides as well as Hides 19 and 20 overlook shallow-water lagoons and areas of bare mud which are well suited to the needs of wading birds. Most feed by probing with their beaks into the mud to catch small creatures; some waders have long legs enabling them to feed in deeper water areas, and long beaks for getting deep down into the mud. Other wading birds have short legs and beaks and feed on bare mud or shallow-water areas. .

For information on which wading birds are present at Welney, consult the information board by the observatory.

SEASONS AT WELNEY

**Welney's Summer
Scene –
A Diorama**

Welney's Summer Scene

For a window of time when the wintering birds have departed for their breeding grounds in the far north and the icy winds of winter have given way to warm summer days, visitors can explore the thriving wildlife of this wetland paradise.

Other areas of interest at Welney in the Summer

There will always be birds to be seen from the hides during the summer months.Spring migration can continue up until the end of June, and by early August the autumn migration will have started.

Many pairs of swallows make their nests of mud inside the hides and if you are not too close will continue to feed insects to their young, unconcerned over your presence. House Martins and swifts, nesting under the eaves and in the roof spaces of cottages out in the Fens, will come to feed on the wealth of insect life at Welney. Flying low over the washes catching insects will be the Sand Martin.

FROM RUSSIA WITH LOVE!

Adopt a Swan Today

Each Autumn the first Bewick's Swans begin to arrive from Arctic Russia at Welney and some of the other Wetland Trust Centres. Thanks to research led by our founder, Sir Peter Scott, we now know that Bewick's Swans pair for life and some loving 'husbands and wives' have been returning from this distant land to our Centres for 20 winters or more.

If you care about these graceful, beautiful birds, why not express your interest by adopting either a Bewick's or a Whooper Swan?

You can adopt a swan and learn its family history. Or you can make a gift to a relative, friend or nature loving colleague.:Whichever way you take one of these magnificent birds under your wing, you'll be making a valuable contribution to the work of The Wildfowl & Wetlands Trust, work dedicated to ensuring that your swan, and flocks of other species (many of them endangered) will always enjoy a healthy, hospitable and safe winter habitat here in Britain. For information on these two kinds of Swan please refer to the earlier section on pages 1V and V.

Swans can be adopted by contacting Welney using the address and telephone number given at the front and back of this section.They can also be adopted by contacting The Bird Adoption Office,WWT, Slimbridge, Glos GL2 7BT Tel (01453 890 333)

Your adoption fee will help WWT to:

1. Maintain the grounds which provide a home for the birds
2. Create new habitats and manage wild reserves for wintering wildfowl
3. Carry out important research into birds
4. Feed and care for the birds at WWT Centres

Benefits of being an adopter are:

1. A personal certificate recording the adoption
2. A photocard showing your type of swan with detailed information about the species
3. A personal handbook containing special offers when visiting our eight Centres
4. Swan News- a newsletter detailing swan sightings
5. Making an imaginative and continuing contribution to help protect wild birds
6. A unique way to build on a child's love of nature and involve them directly in conservation
7. Portrait of your swan.

Swan adoptions are £25 and come with a drawing of the bill pattern and personal history of your adopted swan plus vouchers to see swans at WWT Centres.

The continued existence of the world's wildfowl depends on your action to help conserve them....!
Other birds can also be adopted ie Mallards,Teal,Pochard, Tufted duck and Barnacle and Nene Geese.

NEW CENTRE IN THE HEART OF LONDON!

The Wetland Centre – A vision of London's premier wetland

The past

The Wetland Centre is being created from four former reservoirs which were no longer required thanks to the introduction of The Thames Water Ring Main. The reservoirs had become very important for migratory and resident birds and were designated a Site of Special Scientific Interest (SSSI) in 1975. As it was not practical to maintain these reservoirs, it was decided by Thames Water to find a sympathetic use for the land and today's scheme was developed in conjunction with WWT. The creation of the Wetland Centre is funded through the sale of new homes built by Berkeley Homes on part of the site.

The present

Originally conceived by Sir Peter Scott, founder of The Wildfowl & Wetlands Trust, The Wetland Centre has been a co-operative project by WWT ecologists, landscape architects Scott-Wilson Resource Consultants, consulting engineers Lewin Fryer and Partners, civil engineers Cinnamond Reclamation Ltd and Thames Water. The buildings have been designed by architects John Thompson and Partners. Wildlife monitoring is being supported by English Nature, WWF and the Environment Agency.

Gradually all the reservoirs have been broken up, to be replaced by a complex of lakes, ponds, reedbeds and shallow flooded wetlands. This phase of the work has been completed, with planting continuing for the next two years. Construction work on the Peter Scott Centre commences in 1997 and it is expected that The Wetland Centre will open to the public in the year 2000.

This innovative urban development will create an oasis for wetland wildlife just four miles from Hyde Park Corner.

The future

1. Visitors will be able to see scores of wild birds in beautiful and accessible surroundings as well as being able to find out more about the environment. The latest technology will be used, including a fibre optic cabling system part sponsored by Telewest Communications (London South) Ltd

2. This will relay pictures of nesting and feeding birds on the reserve to screens in the Peter Scott Centre.

3. WWT is also seeking additional funding to add to the educational value of The Wetland Centre.

Plans include:

4. Thames Riverlife-the story of the wildlife of the Thames from source to sea,

5. An Ecodome-a temperature-controlled building interpreting tropical wetlands, and

6. A conservation centre- with facilities for environmental training and community use.

7. The Wetland Centre will include superb facilities like the Peter Scott Centre with restaurant, gift shop, audio-visual theatre and observatory, exhibits on wetlands of the world and many bird hides.

WHERE
to find us

**Headquarters &
National Centre**

Slimbridge
Gloucester GL2 7BT
Tel: (01453) 890333

Regional Centres

Arundel
Mill Road
Arundel
Sussex BN18 9PB
Tel: (01903) 883355

Caerlaverock
Eastpark Farm
Caerlaverock
Dumfriesshire SG1 4RS
Tel: (0138 777) 200

Castle Espie
78 Ballydrain Road
Comber
County Down BT23 6EA
Tel: (01247) 874146

Llanelli
Penclacwydd
Llwynhendy
Llanelli
Dyfed SA14 9SH
Tel: (01554) 741087

Martin Mere
Burscough
Ormskirk
Lancashire L40 0TA
Tel: (01704) 895181

Washington
District 15
Washington
Tyne & Wear NE38 8LE
Tel: (0191) 4165454

Welney
Hundred Foot Bank
Welney, Nr. Wisbech
Cambridgeshire PE14 9TN
Tel: (01353) 860711

A Centre for the future

Barn Elms
Barn Elms Lodge
Queen Elizabeth Walk
Barnes
London SW1 0DB
Tel: (0181) 8768995

Reg. charity no. 1030884

THE POET

Richard Bonfield was born in Leicester in 1959, but now lives in his adopted city, Norwich.

He graduated from The University of East Anglia with an Honours Degree in Development Studies in 1980 and has subsequently found intermittent employment as Jack of all Trades and Master of none.

He has variously been a student, An Advertising Manager for Cover, (Norwich's first equivalent of Time Out), a satirical columnist, a wholefood worker, a C.N.D. publicity officer, the assistant manager of an off licence, a bookshop worker and a caterer. At the present moment in time he is gainfully employed in Oxfam as a voluntary worker specialising in books and records. (A pig in clover in other words).

The success of his first collection **A Bestiary – an Animal Alphabet** has not altered him in any way and has produced no discernible change in either his bank balance or psychological profile.

He is still a committed vegetarian, his poetry continues to be published in a wide variety of magazines, he is still trying to follow the Buddha's eightfold path and he is currently working on that intransigent third collection.

He has just obtained his own council flat and lives there in an Englishman's council flat is his castle sort of a way with his best cat Paddy, although he can often be found round at his girlfriend's entertaining three other favoured felines Mozzie, Jasper and Chino and a vacuum cleaner called Henry.

As far as his hobbies are concerned they still include cider, Zen, Jackson Browne, Van Morrison and gourmet vegetarian cooking plus ad lib piano playing; although they have recently expanded to include acoustic music, amateur theatricals, shopping in Sainsbury's, Mongolian clog dancing and naive painting (eg the cover of the present volume). Sadly he no longer possesses even a Minor Morris.

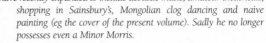

On his mother's side he is, reputedly descended from Robert the Bruce and his father's ancestors hail from Bonneville in France thereby making his full name (Richard Norton Bonfield) something of a Triumph...!

Anyone doubting his claims regarding the Bruce need only compare the shape of the skull pictured opposite with the shape of Robert the Bruce's skull in Edinburgh castle. It must also be said, in his defence that he supports Scottish Home rule, loves caves and has never suffered from Arachnaphobia!